Christmas Candy

Christmas Candy

AVENEL BOOKS
New York

Copyright © 1990 by Outlet Book Company, Inc.

First published in 1990 by Avenel Books,
distributed by Outlet Book Company, Inc.,
a Random House Company,
225 Park Avenue South,
New York, New York 10003

Manufactured in Italy

Edited by Glorya Hale
Designed by Melissa Ring

Library of Congress Cataloging-in-Publication Data

Christmas candy / [edited by Glorya Hale].
p.   cm.
ISBN 0-517-02423-3
1. Candy.   2. Christmas cookery.   I. Hale, Glorya.
TX791.C555   1990   641.8′53—dc20   90-36794   CIP

8   7   6   5   4   3   2

Contents

Introduction

Rich, chewy caramels and luscious creamy fudge, light fluffy divinity and nut-studded brittles, bright candied fruit and crunchy spiced nuts, sweet taffy apples and sumptuous chocolate truffles—these are some of the marvelous confections of Christmas, and you can make them right in your own kitchen.

Making candy is very satisfying, and homemade candy is especially delicious. Candy keeps well and travels well. Packed in a decorative tin, a pretty box, a beribboned jar, or, perhaps, a cut-glass dish, it makes a special gift, even for people who live far away. Homemade candy can be tucked into Christmas stockings. It is wonderful to nibble on while trimming the tree. And nothing is more fun during the holidays than an old-fashioned taffy pull.

This is a new collection of easy-to-follow recipes for a variety of scrumptious treats. (And, other than an inexpensive candy thermometer, no special equipment is required.) There are simple recipes for such old favorites as peppermint creams, almond toffee coated with chocolate, pralines, rocky road, and butterscotch drops. You'll find instructions for making such delights as candied kumquats and candied orange peel, fruit chews, walnut date slices, sugar and spice nuts, and popcorn balls. You'll want to try them all—and make your own candy not only for the holidays, but all through the year.

Making the Best Candy

Candy is not difficult to make. Some of the recipes in this book require little or no cooking. Others need only careful timing and adequate beating. For some types of candy, however, special care is necessary. Follow these basic instructions and you can become a successful and versatile candymaker.

♣ Always read a recipe through from beginning to end before starting to cook.

♣ Always use the best-quality, freshest ingredients available.

♣ Measure ingredients accurately, using standard measuring spoons for small amounts, a fluid measuring cup for liquids, and graduated measuring cups for dry ingredients.

♣ Follow recipes carefully. Use only the ingredients specified and add them in the order and by the method given.

♣ To prevent sugaring, carefully follow directions about stirring and about covering the pan.

♣ Use moderate or low heat, according to instructions in the recipe, so the syrup does not reach the boiling point too quickly.

♣ Always use a saucepan large enough to allow space for the candy to bubble up when boiling. A 2-quart pan is large enough in most cases, but sometimes a 3-quart or even a 4-quart pan is preferable. A pan in which candy is made should be of heavy-gauge metal, which holds heat evenly and will prevent sticking.

♣ Candymaking involves a lot of stirring and beating. Although an electric mixer may be used in some stages of preparation, such as beating egg whites for divinity, for most candy mixtures a spoon is best. A long-handled wooden spoon is preferable, since it will never get too hot to handle.

♣ A candy thermometer that clips onto the side of the pan is almost a necessity for successful candymaking, since it is critical that the candy be removed from the heat at the moment it reaches the proper temperature. It is best to use a clearly marked, easy-to-read thermometer with a mercury ball that is set low enough to measure the temperature of the boiling syrup, but does not touch the bottom of the pan.

To use a candy thermometer, be sure it is at room temperature before putting it into the hot syrup. Lower the thermometer gradually into the candy mixture *after* the sugar is dissolved and the syrup has begun to boil.

♠ The cold-water test is an alternative to a candy thermometer. Many cooks still rely upon this test, although it is not as accurate as a candy thermometer. (All the recipes in this book specify a temperature reading as well as the cold-water test results, such as hard ball or soft ball.)

Temperature Tests for Candy

Temperature of Syrup	Test	Description of Syrup When Dropped Into Very Cold Water
234° to 240°F	Soft ball	Forms a soft ball that flattens on removal from water
244° to 248°F	Firm ball	Forms a firm ball that does not flatten on removal from water
250° to 266°F	Hard ball	Forms a hard ball that, on removal from water, remains hard enough to hold its shape, yet is pliable
270° to 290°F	Soft crack	Separates into threads that are hard, but not brittle, when removed from water
300° to 310°F	Hard crack	Separates into threads that are hard and very brittle

To water-test, use very cold, but not ice, water. Use a clean cup, spoon, and fresh water for each test. Remove the pan from

the heat and drop a little of the hot mixture into the water. Use your fingers to gather the drops into a ball and feel its consistency. If the candy is not yet ready, immediately return the pan to the heat.

🌲 Avoid making candy on damp or rainy days. High humidity is the candymaker's enemy. If for any reason you cannot postpone a candymaking session, cook the candy 1 or 2 degrees higher on the thermometer than indicated in the recipe.

🌲 Altitude also affects candymaking. Temperatures given in recipes in this book are for sea level. At high altitudes the candy must be cooked about 2 degrees higher.

🌲 Be patient and always allow sufficient time. Most candy does take time to make, and there is no way to rush the cooking without disaster.

Storing Candy

One of the nicest things about homemade candy is that it can be eaten when it is at its freshest. In addition, it contains no chemicals, artificial flavoring, or preservatives, although the lack of preservatives does limit its storage capabilities. Most homemade candy, however, will keep well for several weeks if it is stored properly. (The exception is divinity, which gets stale quickly and should be eaten within two days of preparation.) Here are some rules for storing candy successfully.

♣ Sticky and chewy candies, like taffy, nougat, and caramels, and hard candies, like butterscotch, should be individually wrapped in waxed paper, plastic wrap, or foil.

♣ All candy keeps best in an airtight container in a cool, dry place. Some chocolate candies, like truffles, are best stored in the refrigerator.

♣ Do not store brittle candies in the same container with soft, creamy candies. The moisture from the soft candies may make the hard candies sticky.

♣ Candy freezes well. Place the candy, individually wrapped if appropriate, in a cardboard box or plastic container. Overwrap the container with freezer paper or foil. To thaw the candy, let it stand for several hours, or overnight, and come to room temperature before opening the container. This will prevent moisture from collecting on the candies because of the temperature change.

Packaging Candy
and Other Confections

Homemade confections make splendid gifts, and wrapped imaginatively they can be a very special present for a neighbor, a host or hostess, or a friend.

Attractive tins and wooden or cardboard boxes make fine gift containers for candy. When using a round wooden box or tin, first line it with several layers of white doilies. Cut several rounds of waxed paper, a little smaller than the circumference of the box. Arrange the candy on the doilies in the box, then place several thicknesses of waxed paper, then a doily, on top. Tie a ribbon crosswise around the closed box. This would be a nice way to present peanut or cashew brittle or sugar and spice nuts.

Fudge squares are best packed in a square box. Each square can be put into a foil or paper candy cup. Use square doilies to line the box and several thicknesses of waxed paper between layers of the candy.

A wide-mouthed glass jar that has a well-fitting lid can be filled with an assortment of wrapped caramels or taffy, or, perhaps, with candied orange peel. Wrap the jar using several layers of colored tissue paper. Gather the tissue paper at the top with curling ribbon.

A shiny, decorative tin pail is an excellent container for popcorn balls or almond pecan popcorn. Pack the popcorn in a large plastic bag before putting it into the pail. Then put the lid on the pail, seal it with transparent tape, and tie a big, bright bow on top.

When packaging chocolate candies, such as truffles, bourbon balls, or chocolate walnut drops, put each piece into a foil or paper candy cup before putting it into a gift box.

Chocolate Delights

Chocolate bourbon balls, rocky road, chocolate walnut drops, a variety of truffles—these chocolate treats are exceptionally easy to make. Many of them need no cooking, and none of them requires a candy thermometer or cold-water test. Be sure, however, to use the best-quality chocolate available and when melting the chocolate to do so in the top of a double boiler over barely simmering water.

Rocky Road

Chocolate, marshmallows, nuts, and coconut combine to make this the richest and best-ever rocky road. If you are going to include this candy in a gift box, put each square in a foil candy cup.

2 cups semisweet chocolate chips
$2\frac{1}{4}$ cups miniature marshmallows
$\frac{1}{4}$ cup flaked coconut
$\frac{1}{2}$ cup coarsely chopped walnuts

Line an 8-inch square pan with foil. Grease the foil with butter.

In the top of a double boiler, melt the chocolate over barely simmering water, stirring constantly.

Remove from the hot water and stir in the marshmallows, coconut, and walnuts.

Pour the candy into the prepared pan and, using a spatula, spread it into an even layer. Chill in the refrigerator for about 3 hours, or until the candy is firm.

Remove the candy from the pan. Peel off the foil and, using a sharp knife, cut the candy into 1-inch squares.

Chocolate Nut Truffles

The secret of successful truffles is the quality of the chocolate. Always use the best chocolate available. Truffles should be stored in a covered container in the refrigerator. They will keep for about two weeks. Serve them at room temperature.

>   8 ounces semisweet chocolate
>   6 tablespoons unsalted butter
> $\frac{1}{2}$ cup heavy cream
>   1 teaspoon vanilla extract
> $\frac{1}{2}$ cup finely chopped almonds

In the top of a double boiler, melt the chocolate and the butter over barely simmering water, stirring constantly. Remove from the hot water and set aside.

In a small, heavy saucepan, bring the cream just to the boil. Remove from the heat and pour the cream into the chocolate mixture. Mix well. Add the vanilla and stir until the mixture is smooth. Pour into a shallow bowl and set aside to cool, stirring occasionally.

Cover the bowl and chill in the refrigerator for about 4 hours, or until the mixture is firm, but not solid.

Spread the chopped nuts on a plate. Scoop up the chocolate mixture with a teaspoon and shape it into rough balls. Roll the balls in the nuts.

Chocolate Rum Truffles

These truffles are sinfully rich—and very satisfying. Grand Marnier or Kahlúa may be substituted for the rum. Store the truffles, covered, in the refrigerator. Let them stand at room temperature for about 30 minutes before serving.

  2 tablespoons heavy cream
  2 tablespoons dark rum
  6 ounces dark sweet chocolate, coarsely chopped
  4 tablespoons unsalted butter, cut into chunks
  $\frac{1}{2}$ cup unsweetened cocoa powder

In a small, heavy pan, bring the cream just to a boil. Remove the pan from the heat and stir in the rum and the chocolate. Cook over very low heat, stirring constantly, until the chocolate melts.

Remove the pan from the heat and quickly mix the butter into the chocolate mixture. When the butter has melted and the mixture is smooth, pour it into a shallow bowl and set aside to cool. Cover the bowl and chill in the refrigerator for about 2 hours, or until the mixture is firm enough to handle.

Sift the cocoa onto a large plate. Scoop up the chocolate mixture with a teaspoon and shape it into rough balls. Roll each ball in the cocoa.

Milk Chocolate Truffles

Lightly spiced with cinnamon, these milk chocolate truffles are sweet, rich, and creamy. Store them covered in the refrigerator, but serve them at room temperature.

6 ounces milk chocolate
$\frac{1}{2}$ teaspoon ground cinnamon
$1\frac{1}{2}$ teaspoons unsalted butter, at room temperature
$\frac{1}{2}$ cup less 1 teaspoon sweetened condensed milk
$\frac{1}{2}$ teaspoon vanilla extract
$\frac{1}{2}$ cup chocolate sprinkles

In the top of a double boiler, melt the chocolate over barely simmering water, stirring constantly.

Remove from the hot water and stir in the cinnamon and the butter. When the butter is melted and the mixture is smooth, add the condensed milk and the vanilla. Stir until well blended.

Pour the mixture into a shallow bowl. Cover the bowl and chill in the refrigerator for 3 hours, or until the mixture is firm enough to handle.

Spread the chocolate sprinkles on a large plate. Scoop up the chocolate mixture with a teaspoon and shape it into balls. Roll each ball in the chocolate sprinkles.

Double Chocolate Delights

This luscious candy is extremely easy to make. It should be stored in a covered container in the refrigerator.

    8 *ounces unsweetened chocolate*
    4 *ounces German's sweet chocolate*
  15 *ounce can sweetened condensed milk*
    1 *cup finely chopped pecans*

In the top of a double boiler, melt the chocolates over barely simmering water, stirring constantly. Add the condensed milk and stir until well blended. Remove from the hot water. Pour the mixture into a shallow bowl and set aside to cool.

Cover the bowl and chill in the refrigerator for 1 hour, or until the mixture is firm enough to handle.

Spread the chopped nuts on a large plate. Scoop up the chocolate mixture with a teaspoon and shape it into balls. Roll each ball in the nuts.

Chocolate Bourbon Balls

These delicious candies require no cooking and will keep well in an airtight container in a cool place. Whiskey, rum, or your favorite liquor may be substituted for the bourbon.

    1 *cup chocolate-wafer cookie crumbs*
    2 *cups coarsely chopped pecans*
    1 *cup confectioners' sugar*
  $1\frac{1}{2}$ *tablespoons light corn syrup*
    $\frac{1}{4}$ *cup bourbon*

In a blender or food processor, coarsely grind the cookie

crumbs with 1 cup of the pecans. Transfer to a large mixing bowl. Add the sugar, corn syrup, and bourbon and mix thoroughly.

Shape the mixture into 1-inch balls.

Spread the remaining 1 cup of pecans on a plate. Roll the balls in the nuts.

Chocolate Coconut Cups

These elegant candies couldn't be easier to make. After they are firm, they may be stored in an airtight container in a cool, dry place.

  8 *ounces bittersweet chocolate*
  1$\frac{1}{3}$ *cups flaked coconut*

Put 25 foil candy cups on a cookie sheet.

In the top of a double boiler, melt the chocolate over barely simmering water, stirring constantly.

Remove from the hot water and add the coconut. Mix lightly until the coconut is completely coated with the chocolate.

Drop a teaspoonful of the mixture into each foil cup. Chill in the refrigerator until firm.

Chocolate Walnut Drops

These delicious candies are easy to make. They should be stored in an airtight container in a cool, dry place.

> 1 *cup firmly packed dark brown sugar*
> $\frac{1}{3}$ *cup evaporated milk*
> 2 *tablespoons light corn syrup*
> 1 *cup semisweet chocolate chips*
> $\frac{1}{2}$ *cup finely chopped walnuts*
> 1 *teaspoon vanilla extract*
>   *Walnut halves*

Line a cookie sheet with waxed paper.

In a heavy saucepan, combine the sugar, milk, and corn syrup. Cook over moderate heat, stirring constantly, until the sugar is dissolved and the mixture comes to a boil. Boil, stirring constantly, for 2 minutes.

Remove the pan from the heat. Add the chocolate chips, chopped walnuts, and vanilla and stir until the chocolate is melted and the mixture is slightly thickened.

Drop the candy by rounded teaspoonfuls onto the prepared cookie sheet. Press a walnut half on top of each mound.

Chill in the refrigerator for 30 minutes, or until the candies are firm.

Christmas Wishes

Divinity and Other Divine Candies

Light-as-air divinity, pecan-studded pralines, and classic pepper-mint creams are among the delights included here. None of these candies is difficult to make. Some don't require a candy thermometer or cold-water testing. Most of them are drop candies. When dropping these or any candies from a spoon, be sure to work quickly or the mixture may harden in the bowl. Do not attempt to make any of these candies on a humid or rainy day, because, even if the recipes are followed to the letter, the candy will not set properly.

Divinity Kisses

Light and sweet, divinity is a distant cousin of meringue. To make coconut divinity, substitute $\frac{3}{4}$ cup of flaked coconut for the walnuts and omit the cherries.

    $2\frac{1}{2}$ cups granulated sugar
    $\frac{1}{2}$ cup light corn syrup
    $\frac{1}{2}$ cup water
    $\frac{1}{4}$ teaspoon salt
    2 large egg whites, at room temperature
    1 teaspoon vanilla extract
    $\frac{1}{2}$ cup coarsely chopped walnuts
      Red and green candied cherries, halved

Spread a large piece of waxed paper on a work surface.

In a large, heavy saucepan, combine the sugar, corn syrup, water, and salt. Cook over moderate heat, stirring constantly, until the sugar is dissolved. Cover the pan and continue to cook over moderate heat until the mixture comes to a boil, 2 to 3 minutes. Remove the lid and continue cooking, without stirring, until the syrup reaches the hard-ball stage (265°F on a candy thermometer).

While the syrup is cooking, in a large mixing bowl beat the egg whites until stiff peaks form.

Pour the hot syrup into the egg whites in a fine stream, beating constantly and at high speed with an electric mixer. When the mixture becomes thick and heavy, it will be necessary to use a wooden spoon to beat it. Add the vanilla and continue beating until the candy just holds its shape when dropped from the spoon. Quickly stir in the nuts.

Drop the candy by rounded teaspoonfuls onto the waxed paper. Press a candied cherry half into each kiss.

Chocolate Divinity

No candy is as divine as divinity, and for the chocoholic nothing beats chocolate divinity.

    3 tablespoons unsalted butter
    ½ cup unsweetened cocoa powder
    2½ cups granulated sugar
    ½ cup light corn syrup
    ⅓ cup water
    ¼ teaspoon salt
    2 large egg whites
    1 teaspoon vanilla extract
    ¾ cup finely chopped walnuts

Spread a large piece of waxed paper on a work surface.

In the top of a double boiler, melt the butter over hot, not boiling, water. Add the cocoa and stir until smooth. Remove from the hot water and set aside.

In a large, heavy saucepan, combine the sugar, corn syrup, water, and salt. Cook over moderate heat, stirring constantly, until the sugar is dissolved. Cover the pan and continue to cook over moderate heat, until the mixture comes to a boil, 2 to 3 minutes. Remove the lid and continue cooking without stirring, until the syrup reaches the hard-ball stage (265°F on a candy thermometer).

While the syrup is cooking, in a large mixing bowl beat the egg whites until stiff peaks form.

Pour the hot syrup into the egg whites in a fine stream, beating constantly and at high speed with an electric mixer. When the mixture becomes thick and heavy, it will be necessary to use a wooden spoon to beat it. Add the vanilla and continue beating until the candy just holds its shape when dropped from the spoon. Quickly blend in the cocoa mixture, then the nuts.

Drop the candy by teaspoonfuls onto the waxed paper.

Divinity Squares

These divinity squares are topped with chocolate and chopped walnuts—and they are very special.

2½ cups granulated sugar
½ cup light corn syrup
½ cup water
¼ teaspoon salt
2 large egg whites, at room temperature
1 teaspoon vanilla extract
2 ounces semisweet chocolate
¾ cup finely chopped walnuts

Grease an 8-inch square pan with butter.

In a large, heavy saucepan, combine the sugar, corn syrup, water, and salt. Cook over moderate heat, stirring constantly, until the sugar is dissolved. Cover the pan and continue to cook over moderate heat until the mixture comes to a boil, 2 to 3 minutes. Remove the lid and continue cooking, without stirring, until the mixture reaches the hard-ball stage (265°F on a candy thermometer).

While the syrup is cooking, in a large mixing bowl beat the egg whites until stiff peaks form.

Pour the hot syrup into the egg whites in a fine stream, beating constantly and at high speed with an electric mixer. When the mixture becomes thick and heavy it will be necessary to use a wooden spoon to beat it. Add the vanilla and continue beating until the candy just holds its shape when dropped from the spoon.

Spoon the divinity into the prepared pan. Using a rubber spatula, smooth it into an even layer.

In the top of a double boiler, melt the chocolate over barely simmering water, stirring constantly. Remove from the hot water and set aside to cool.

Pour the cooled melted chocolate over the divinity and spread in an even layer with a clean rubber spatula. Sprinkle the chopped nuts over the chocolate.

When the candy has cooled completely, use a sharp knife to cut it into squares.

Coconut Cherry Patties

Top these creamy patties with red and green candied cherry halves for a festive look. If you prefer, you can substitute pecan or walnut halves.

2 cups granulated sugar
$\frac{1}{2}$ cup milk
1$\frac{1}{2}$ cups flaked coconut
1 teaspoon vanilla extract
    Red and green candied cherries, halved

Spread a large sheet of waxed paper on a work surface.

In a heavy saucepan combine the sugar and the milk. Cook over high heat, stirring constantly, until the sugar is dissolved. Reduce the heat to moderate and cook, stirring constantly, until the mixture reaches the soft-ball stage (238°F on a candy thermometer).

Remove the pan from the heat and stir in the coconut and the vanilla.

Drop the candy by teaspoonfuls, about 2 inches apart, onto the waxed paper. With a spatula flatten each mound. Place half a candied cherry in the center of each patty.

Maple Pecan Candy

This luscious, creamy candy takes about 20 minutes to make—
and it's so easy you don't even need a candy thermometer.

4 cups pure maple syrup
1 cup heavy cream
¼ cup unsalted butter
1 cup coarsely chopped pecans
1 teaspoon lemon extract

Liberally grease an 8-inch square pan with butter.

In a heavy saucepan, combine the maple syrup, cream, and
butter. Cook over moderate heat, stirring constantly, until the
mixture comes to a boil. Continue cooking for 9 minutes, stirring frequently.

Remove the pan from the heat. Stir in the pecans and the
lemon extract. Stir for 5 minutes.

Pour the candy into the prepared pan. When it is completely
cool, cut it into squares.

 26

Pralines

A praline studded with pecans is a perennial favorite. If you like large patties, drop the pralines from a tablespoon. If you prefer them smaller, use a teaspoon. When the pralines have cooled completely, they may be stored in an airtight container between layers of waxed paper.

4 *cups firmly packed light brown sugar*
$\frac{2}{3}$ *cup half-and-half*
2 *tablespoons unsalted butter*
$\frac{1}{8}$ *teaspoon salt*
2 *cups coarsely chopped pecans*

Spread a large sheet of waxed paper on a work surface.

In a large, heavy saucepan combine the sugar, half-and-half, butter, and salt. Cook over high heat, stirring constantly until the sugar is dissolved.

Reduce the heat to moderate and continue cooking, without stirring, until the mixture comes to a boil. In the meantime, fill with water a pan into which the saucepan will fit. Bring the water to a boil, then turn off the heat.

When the mixture comes to a boil, begin stirring constantly. Boil for 4 minutes, then stir in the nuts.

Put the saucepan over the hot water while dropping the candy from a spoon onto the waxed paper.

Peppermint Creams

These creamy candies look quite pretty when red or green food coloring is added.

2 *cups granulated sugar*
$\frac{1}{4}$ *cup light corn syrup*
$\frac{1}{4}$ *cup milk*
$\frac{1}{4}$ *teaspoon cream of tartar*
$\frac{1}{2}$ *teaspoon peppermint flavoring*
   Red or green food coloring

Spread a large sheet of waxed paper on a work surface.

In a heavy saucepan, combine the sugar, corn syrup, milk, and cream of tartar. Cook over low heat, stirring constantly, until the sugar is dissolved.

Increase the heat to moderate and continue cooking, stirring constantly, until the mixture reaches the soft-ball stage (238°F on a candy thermometer). Remove the pan from the heat and set aside for about 3 minutes to allow the mixture to cool slightly.

Beat in the peppermint and a few drops of food coloring. Continue beating until the mixture is creamy.

Drop the candy by teaspoonfuls onto the waxed paper.

Brittles and Butterscotch

Peanut brittle, cashew brittle, and an unusual fruit and nut brittle are featured in this section along with a wonderful chocolate-coated almond toffee and old-fashioned butterscotch drops. Each of these candies should be cooked in a large pan because the syrup will boil up as it cooks. They all require quite a bit of cooking time, but the results are well worth it.

Peanut Brittle

Peanut brittle is a traditional favorite. It is not difficult to make, but be sure to use a large saucepan, preferably a 3-quart pan, because it will boil up.

> 1 *cup granulated sugar*
> $\frac{1}{2}$ *cup light corn syrup*
> 2 *tablespoons unsalted butter*
> $\frac{1}{2}$ *cup water*
> $\frac{1}{2}$ *teaspoon salt*
> $1\frac{1}{2}$ *cups unsalted peanuts*
> 1 *teaspoon baking soda*

Liberally grease a large cookie sheet with butter.

Grease the sides of a large, heavy saucepan with butter. In the pan combine the sugar, corn syrup, butter, water, and salt. Cook over moderate heat, stirring constantly, until the sugar is dissolved and the mixture comes to a boil. Stir in the peanuts. Continue cooking, stirring frequently, until the mixture reaches the hard-crack stage (300°F on a candy thermometer).

Remove the pan from the heat and vigorously stir in the baking soda.

Immediately pour the candy onto the prepared cookie sheet.

Using two forks, lift and pull the candy into a rectangle about $\frac{1}{2}$ inch thick.

When the brittle is completely cool, break it into pieces.

I wish you a Merry Xmas,
And mirth without measure,
A festive board well laden,
With many an Xmas pleasure.

Cashew Brittle

More elegant than peanut brittle, this cashew brittle is just as easy to prepare and it makes a wonderful Christmas gift since it keeps extremely well in an airtight container.

2 cups granulated sugar
1 cup light corn syrup
1 cup unsalted butter
$\frac{1}{2}$ cup water
3 cups unsalted cashew nuts, coarsely chopped
$1\frac{1}{2}$ teaspoons baking soda

Liberally grease 2 large cookie sheets with butter.

Grease the sides of a large, heavy saucepan with butter. In the pan combine the sugar, corn syrup, butter, and water. Cook over moderate heat, stirring constantly, until the sugar is dissolved and the mixture comes to a boil. Continue cooking, stirring occasionally, until the mixture reaches the soft-crack stage (275°F on a candy thermometer). Stir in the cashew nuts. Continue cooking, stirring frequently, until the mixture reaches the hard-crack stage (300°F).

Remove the pan from the heat and vigorously stir in the baking soda.

Immediately pour half the candy onto each prepared cookie sheet. Using two forks, pull the candy into rectangles about $\frac{1}{2}$ inch thick.

When the brittle is completely cool, break it into pieces.

Fruit and Nut Brittle

This is an unusual candy—a brittle rich with nuts, coconut, and fruit and flavored with lemon. It is a nice change from traditional nut brittles.

$\frac{1}{2}$ cup thinly sliced Brazil nuts
$\frac{1}{4}$ cup raisins
$\frac{1}{4}$ cup chopped dried apricots
$\frac{1}{4}$ cup flaked coconut
2 cups granulated sugar
2 tablespoons unsalted butter
$\frac{1}{4}$ cup white vinegar
$\frac{1}{4}$ cup water
1 teaspoon lemon extract

Liberally grease a 9-inch square pan with butter.

In a mixing bowl, combine the nuts, raisins, apricots, and coconut. Mix well, then make a layer of the mixture in the prepared pan. Set aside.

Grease the sides of a large, heavy saucepan with butter. In the pan combine the sugar, butter, vinegar, and water. Cook over moderate heat, stirring constantly, until the sugar is dissolved. Continue cooking, stirring frequently, until the mixture reaches the soft-crack stage (270°F on a candy thermometer).

Remove the pan from the heat and stir in the lemon extract. Pour the hot syrup over the fruit and nuts in the pan.

When the brittle is completely cool, break it into pieces.

Almond Toffee

Buttery and coated with chocolate, this candy should be stored in an airtight container with waxed paper between the layers.

2 cups granulated sugar
1¼ cups light corn syrup
1 cup unsalted butter
½ cup water
2¾ cups finely chopped almonds
2 cups semisweet chocolate chips

Liberally grease two 8-inch square pans with butter.

Grease the sides of a large, heavy saucepan with butter. In the pan, combine the sugar, corn syrup, butter, and water. Cook over moderate heat, stirring constantly, until the sugar is dissolved and the mixture comes to a boil. Continue cooking, stirring occasionally, until the mixture reaches the hard-crack stage (300°F on a candy thermometer).

Immediately remove the pan from the heat and stir in 1¾ cups of the almonds.

Pour half of the candy into each of the prepared pans. Sprinkle 1 cup of the chocolate chips over the hot toffee in each pan. Using a spatula, spread the chocolate so there is an even layer on top of the toffee. Sprinkle the remaining chopped almonds over the chocolate.

When the toffee is completely cool, break it into pieces.

Butterscotch Drops

These old-fashioned butterscotch candies are better than any butterscotch you can buy in a store. Be sure to cook the candy in a deep kettle or a 4-quart saucepan, because it will foam up as it boils.

2 cups firmly packed dark brown sugar
$\frac{1}{4}$ cup molasses
$\frac{1}{2}$ cup unsalted butter
2 tablespoons water
2 tablespoons white vinegar

Spread a large sheet of waxed paper on a work surface.

In a large, deep kettle, combine the sugar, molasses, butter, water, and vinegar. Cook over moderate heat, stirring constantly, until the sugar is dissolved and the mixture comes to a boil. Let the mixture boil hard, stirring frequently with a long-handled wooden spoon, until it reaches the hard-crack stage (300°F on a candy thermometer).

Drop the candy by teaspoonfuls onto the waxed paper.

When the butterscotch drops are completely cool, wrap each one in plastic wrap.

Fudge Favorites

Everyone loves fudge, and here is a collection of marvelous fudge recipes. There's old-fashioned chocolate fudge, penuche, fruit fudge, an unusual banana walnut fudge, never-fail recipes for creamy chocolate pecan fudge and butterscotch walnut fudge, and a rich mocha fudge that requires no cooking.

When making any old-fashioned fudge, use a candy thermometer and be sure to watch the temperatures carefully. When the mixture reaches the boiling point, it becomes very sensitive to stirring and beating. Follow the recipes carefully and success is ensured.

Old-Fashioned Chocolate Fudge

This traditional, rich chocolate fudge is not difficult to make. Just follow the instructions carefully and be sure to use a candy thermometer.

> 2 *ounces unsweetened chocolate*
> 1 *cup milk*
> 2 *cups granulated sugar*
> 1 *tablespoon light corn syrup*
> 2 *tablespoons unsalted butter, at room temperature*
> 1 *teaspoon vanilla extract*
> $\frac{1}{2}$ *cup finely chopped walnuts*

Grease an 8-inch square pan with butter.

In a large, heavy saucepan, combine the chocolate and the milk. Cook over low heat, stirring constantly, until the chocolate has melted and the mixture is smooth.

Stir in the sugar and corn syrup. Increase the heat to moderate and continue stirring until the mixture comes to a boil.

Cover the pan and cook for 1 minute. Uncover the pan and insert a candy thermometer. Cook, uncovered, without stirring, until the mixture reaches the soft-ball stage (236°F on the candy thermometer).

Remove the pan from the heat and stir in the butter and the vanilla. Set aside until the candy cools to lukewarm (110°F).

With a wooden spoon, beat the fudge until it is thick and creamy and no longer glossy. Quickly stir in the nuts.

Pour the fudge into the prepared pan. Cool in the pan on a wire rack.

When the fudge is firm and completely cool, cut it into squares.

Penuche

A brown-sugar fudge studded with pecans, penuche has a creamy texture and caramel flavor.

2 cups firmly packed dark brown sugar
¾ cup milk
⅛ teaspoon salt
¼ cup unsalted butter, at room temperature
1 teaspoon vanilla extract
1 cup coarsely chopped pecans

Grease an 8-inch square pan with butter.

In a large, heavy saucepan, combine the sugar, milk, and salt. Cook over moderate heat, stirring constantly, until the mixture comes to a boil. Continue cooking, without stirring, to the soft-ball stage (236°F on the candy thermometer).

Remove the pan from the heat and stir in the butter and the vanilla. Set aside until the candy cools to lukewarm (110°F).

With a wooden spoon, beat the fudge until it becomes thick and begins to lose its gloss. Quickly stir in the pecans.

Pour the fudge into the prepared pan. Cool in the pan on a wire rack.

When the fudge is firm and completely cool, cut it into squares.

Fruit Fudge

This is an old recipe, but it is always successful. Candied cherries may be substituted for the mixed fruit.

2 cups granulated sugar
1 cup milk
$\frac{1}{4}$ cup unsalted butter
1 teaspoon vanilla extract
$\frac{1}{2}$ cup mixed candied fruit, coarsely chopped

Grease an 8-inch square pan with butter.

In a large, heavy saucepan, combine the sugar, milk, and butter. Cook over high heat, stirring constantly, until the sugar is dissolved. Reduce the heat to moderate and continue to cook, stirring constantly, until the mixture comes to a boil.

Cover the pan and cook for 1 minute. Uncover the pan and insert a candy thermometer. Cook, uncovered, without stirring, until the mixture reaches the soft-ball stage (236°F on the candy thermometer).

Remove the pan from the heat and stir in the vanilla. Set aside until the candy cools to lukewarm (110°F).

With a wooden spoon, beat the fudge until it is thick and creamy and is no longer glossy. Quickly stir in the fruit.

Pour the fudge into the prepared pan. Cool in the pan on a wire rack.

When the fudge is firm and completely cool, cut it into squares.

Banana Walnut Fudge

This firm fudge is nicely spiced with cinnamon. It is an old and unusual recipe. A candy thermometer will ensure success.

2 large, ripe bananas
$2\frac{1}{2}$ cups granulated sugar
$\frac{1}{2}$ cup firmly packed dark brown sugar
1 cup milk
$\frac{1}{2}$ teaspoon cream of tartar
2 tablespoons unsalted butter
$\frac{1}{4}$ teaspoon salt
$\frac{1}{2}$ teaspoon ground cinnamon
1 teaspoon vanilla extract
1 cup coarsely chopped walnuts

Grease an 8-inch square pan with butter. Mash the bananas.

In a large, heavy saucepan, combine the mashed bananas, sugars, milk, cream of tartar, butter, salt, and cinnamon. Cook over moderate heat, stirring occasionally, until the mixture reaches 226°F on a candy thermometer. Then stir constantly until it reaches the soft-ball stage (236°F).

Remove the pan from the heat and stir in the vanilla. Using a wooden spoon, beat the fudge only until it starts to become creamy and is no longer glossy. Stir in the nuts.

Quickly spread the fudge in the prepared pan. Cool in the pan on a wire rack.

While the fudge is slightly warm, cut it into squares.

Creamy Chocolate Pecan Fudge

This creamy fudge never fails, and it is very easy to make. It will keep best well-covered in the refrigerator.

   7 ounce jar marshmallow cream
   $1\frac{1}{2}$ cups granulated sugar
   $\frac{2}{3}$ cup evaporated milk
   $\frac{1}{4}$ cup unsalted butter
   $\frac{1}{4}$ teaspoon salt
   3 cups semisweet chocolate chips
   1 teaspoon vanilla extract
   1 cup coarsely chopped pecans

Line an 8-inch square pan with foil.

In a large, heavy saucepan, combine the marshmallow cream, sugar, milk, butter, and salt. Bring to a rolling boil over moderate heat, stirring constantly. Boil the mixture, stirring constantly, for 5 minutes.

Remove the pan from the heat and add the chocolate chips, stirring until they have melted and the mixture is smooth. Add the vanilla and the pecans and mix well.

Pour the fudge into the prepared pan. Using a spatula, smooth the top.

Chill in the refrigerator for 2 hours, or until the fudge is firm. Then turn it out of the pan, remove the foil, and cut the fudge into squares.

Christmas Greetings

Butterscotch Walnut Fudge

This butterscotch fudge is very easy to prepare. You don't even need a candy thermometer. The fudge will keep best well-covered in the refrigerator.

$1\frac{1}{2}$ cups finely chopped walnuts
7 ounce jar marshmallow cream
$1\frac{1}{2}$ cups granulated sugar
$\frac{2}{3}$ cup evaporated milk
$\frac{1}{4}$ cup unsalted butter
$\frac{1}{4}$ teaspoon salt
2 cups butterscotch chips

Line an 8-inch square pan with foil. Spread $\frac{3}{4}$ cup of the walnuts in an even layer on the foil.

In a large, heavy saucepan, combine the marshmallow cream, sugar, milk, butter, and salt. Bring to a rolling boil over moderate heat, stirring constantly. Boil the mixture, stirring constantly, for 5 minutes.

Remove the pan from the heat. Stir in the butterscotch chips. Continue to stir until they have melted and the mixture is smooth.

Pour the fudge into the prepared pan and sprinkle the remaining $\frac{3}{4}$ cup of walnuts evenly on top. Using a rubber spatula, gently press the walnuts into the fudge.

Chill in the refrigerator for 2 hours, or until the fudge is firm. Then turn it out of the pan, remove the foil, and cut the fudge into squares.

Mocha Fudge Slices

This rich fudge requires no cooking. Store the slices, layered with waxed paper, in a covered container in the refrigerator. Let them stand at room temperature for about 20 minutes before serving.

6 ounces unsweetened chocolate
1 tablespoon instant coffee powder
2 teaspoons boiling water
8 ounce package cream cheese, at room temperature
$\frac{1}{2}$ teaspoon ground cinnamon
$\frac{1}{8}$ teaspoon salt
$\frac{1}{4}$ cup coffee liqueur
5 cups sifted confectioners' sugar
$2\frac{1}{2}$ cups finely chopped walnuts

In the top of a double boiler, melt the chocolate over barely simmering water, stirring constantly. Remove from the hot water and set aside to cool.

In a small bowl, dissolve the coffee in the boiling water.

In a large mixing bowl, combine the cream cheese, cinnamon, and salt. Beat until the mixture is smooth. Gradually beat in the liqueur and the coffee. Add the melted chocolate and beat until it is well blended. Add the sugar, 1 cup at a time, beating well after each addition. Add 1 cup of nuts and mix well.

Cover the bowl and chill the fudge in the refrigerator for 1 hour, or until it is firm enough to handle.

Spread the remaining $1\frac{1}{2}$ cups of nuts on a cookie sheet.

Divide the fudge into quarters. Working with one quarter at a time, place the fudge in the center of a 12-inch piece of waxed paper. Fold two opposite sides over the fudge. Roll the wrapped fudge into a log about $1\frac{1}{2}$ inches in diameter. Remove the waxed paper and roll the fudge log in the chopped nuts. Wrap each fudge log in plastic wrap and refrigerate overnight, then cut into $\frac{1}{2}$-inch slices.

Caramels and Taffy

These chewy treats are the perfect candies for holiday gift-giving because they are easy to pack, travel well, and stored in an airtight container will stay fresh for about 6 weeks. Here are recipes for vanilla caramels and chocolate caramels—plain and with pecans—as well as four kinds of taffy. All these candies must be individually wrapped as soon as they have cooled completely. None of them should be made on a damp or humid day, so resist the temptation to have a taffy pull when the weather is bad.

Chocolate Caramels

These candies are creamy, rich, and sweet. They are better than any store-bought caramels.

> 1 cup granulated sugar
> $\frac{3}{4}$ cup light corn syrup
> 3 ounces semisweet chocolate
> $\frac{1}{4}$ teaspoon salt
> $1\frac{1}{2}$ cups heavy cream

Line an 8-inch square pan with foil. Lightly grease the foil with butter.

In a large, heavy saucepan, combine the sugar, corn syrup, chocolate, salt, and $\frac{1}{2}$ cup of the cream. Cook over moderate heat, stirring constantly, until the mixture reaches the soft-ball stage (238°F on a candy thermometer).

Stir in $\frac{1}{2}$ cup of cream and cook, stirring constantly, until the mixture again reaches the soft-ball stage (238°F).

Gradually stir in the remaining $\frac{1}{2}$ cup of cream and continue cooking, without stirring, until the mixture reaches the firm-ball stage (248°F).

Remove the saucepan from the heat and pour the caramel into the prepared pan. Do not scrape the saucepan. Put the pan on a wire rack to cool.

When the caramel is cold and firm, lift it out of the pan and remove the foil. Using a sharp knife, mark it into 1-inch squares, then cut it. Let the caramels dry for about 4 hours, then wrap each one in plastic wrap or waxed paper.

Vanilla Caramels

Walnuts makes these chewy vanilla caramels a special treat.

   2 cups granulated sugar
   2 cups light cream
   1 cup corn syrup
   ½ teaspoon salt
   ⅓ cup unsalted butter, at room temperature
   1 teaspoon vanilla extract
   ½ cup coarsely chopped walnuts

Line an 8-inch square baking pan with foil. Lightly grease the foil with butter.

In a large, heavy saucepan combine the sugar, 1 cup of the cream, the corn syrup, and salt. Cook over moderate heat, stirring constantly, for 10 minutes. In a small saucepan, warm the remaining 1 cup of cream. Add it very slowly to the syrup so it does not stop boiling. Cook, stirring constantly, for 5 minutes.

Stir in the butter, 1 teaspoonful at a time. Continue cooking, stirring constantly, until the candy reaches the firm-ball stage (248°F on a candy thermometer).

Remove the pan from the heat and stir in the vanilla and the nuts.

Pour the caramel into the prepared pan. Do not scrape the saucepan. Put the pan on a wire rack to cool.

When the caramel is cold and firm, lift it out of the pan and remove the foil. Using a sharp knife, mark the carmel into 1-inch squares, then cut it. Let the caramels dry for about 4 hours, then wrap each one in plastic wrap or waxed paper.

Chocolate Pecan Caramels

These caramels are rich—and easy to make. But don't attempt to make them on a rainy or a humid day.

  1 cup unsalted butter
  2¼ cups granulated sugar
  2 ounces unsweetened chocolate
  ¼ teaspoon salt
  1 cup light corn syrup
  1⅓ cups sweetened condensed milk
  ½ teaspoon vanilla extract
  1 cup coarsely chopped pecans

Lightly oil a 9-inch square pan.

In a large, heavy saucepan, melt the butter over very low heat. Add the sugar, chocolate, and salt and cook, stirring constantly, until the chocolate is melted and the ingredients are well blended.

Stir in the corn syrup. Gradually add the milk, stirring constantly.

Increase the heat to moderate and cook, stirring frequently, until the mixture reaches the firm-ball stage (248°F on a candy thermometer).

Remove the pan from the heat and set aside for 5 minutes.

Stir in the vanilla and the nuts and quickly pour the candy into the prepared pan. Put the pan on a wire rack to cool.

When the caramel has cooled to room temperature, turn it out onto a smooth surface. Using a sharp knife, mark the caramel into 1-inch squares, then cut it. Let the caramels dry for about 4 hours, then wrap each one in plastic wrap or waxed paper.

Vanilla Cream Taffy

This taffy has a light, creamy consistency. Remember to pull it with the fingertips rather than the whole hand. If the taffy is too sticky to pull easily, dip the fingers in cornstarch. Store the wrapped taffy in an airtight container in a cool, dry place.

1 cup heavy cream
2 cups granulated sugar
$\frac{1}{4}$ cup light corn syrup
$\frac{3}{4}$ cup water
$\frac{1}{4}$ teaspoon salt
1 teaspoon vanilla extract

Grease a large platter with butter. In a small saucepan, warm the cream. Set it aside.

In a large, heavy saucepan, combine the sugar, corn syrup, water, and salt. Cook over moderate heat, stirring constantly, until the sugar is dissolved. Continue cooking, without stirring, until the mixture just reaches the hard-ball stage (250°F on a candy thermometer).

Add the warm cream and cook over low heat, stirring frequently, until the mixture reaches the hard-ball stage (260°F). Pour the candy onto the prepared platter.

When the taffy is cool enough to handle, in about 10 minutes, pour the vanilla into the center and gather the corners toward it. Remove the taffy from the platter and pull, with fingertips, until it is quite firm and a light cream color.

Stretch the taffy into a long rope about $\frac{3}{4}$ inch in diameter. Using buttered kitchen scissors, cut the rope into 1-inch pieces. Wrap each piece in plastic wrap or waxed paper.

Salt Water Taffy

Atlantic City, New Jersey, is famous for its salt water taffy, which was believed to be made from salt water. Here is the basic recipe. While the taffy is being pulled, it may be colored with food coloring and flavored with a few drops of a flavor extract or oil. Traditionally, pink taffy is flavored with cinnamon or wintergreen, green with spearmint, yellow with lemon, and white with peppermint.

Be sure to pull the taffy only with the fingertips, not with the whole hand. If the taffy is too sticky to handle easily, dip the fingers into cornstarch. When more than one person is going to pull the taffy, grease an appropriate number of platters or pans and divide the taffy among them. Store the wrapped taffy in an airtight container in a cool, dry place.

> 2 *cups granulated sugar*
> $\frac{1}{2}$ *cup light corn syrup*
> $\frac{2}{3}$ *cup water*
> $\frac{1}{8}$ *teaspoon salt*
> 1 *teaspoon vanilla extract*

Grease a large platter with butter.

In a large, heavy saucepan, combine the sugar, corn syrup, water, and salt. Cook over moderate heat, stirring constantly, until the sugar is dissolved. Continue cooking, without stirring, until the mixture reaches the hard-ball stage (262°F on a candy thermometer). Pour the candy onto the prepared platter.

When the taffy is cool enough to handle, pour the vanilla into the center and fold the corners over it. Pull the taffy, with fingertips, until it holds its shape and is light in color.

Stretch the taffy into a long rope about $\frac{3}{4}$ inch in diameter. Using buttered kitchen scissors, cut the rope into 2-inch pieces. Wrap each piece in plastic wrap or waxed paper.

Molasses Taffy

This old-fashioned, golden taffy is a real treat. Make it in a very large saucepan—a 4-quart pan is best—because the molasses mixture will rise quickly and high as it cooks. If the taffy becomes too cool to pull, heat it for 5 minutes in a 350°F oven.

2 cups granulated sugar
1 cup light molasses
1 cup water
1 tablespoon white vinegar
$\frac{1}{8}$ teaspoon salt
$\frac{1}{4}$ cup unsalted butter, at room temperature

Grease a large platter with butter.

In a large, heavy saucepan, combine the sugar, molasses, water, vinegar, and salt. Cook over moderate heat, stirring constantly, until the sugar is dissolved and the mixture comes to a boil.

Reduce the heat to low and continue cooking, stirring frequently, until the mixture reaches the hard-ball stage (262°F on a candy thermometer).

Remove the pan from the heat and stir in the butter. Pour the candy onto the prepared platter.

When the taffy is cool enough to handle, divide it in half and pull each half, with fingertips, until it is quite firm and light in color.

Pull the taffy into a long rope about $\frac{3}{4}$ inch in diameter. Using buttered kitchen scissors, cut the rope into 1-inch pieces. Wrap each piece in plastic wrap or waxed paper.

Chocolate Taffy

Kids love to pull taffy, and everyone will love to eat this taffy—because it's chocolate. If the taffy is too sticky to handle easily, dip the fingers into cornstarch.

$1\frac{1}{4}$ cups granulated sugar
$\frac{3}{4}$ cup light corn syrup
$\frac{1}{3}$ cup unsweetened cocoa powder
$\frac{1}{8}$ teaspoon salt
2 teaspoons white vinegar
$\frac{1}{4}$ cup evaporated milk
1 tablespoon unsalted butter, at room temperature

Liberally grease a large platter with butter.

In a large, heavy saucepan, combine the sugar, corn syrup, cocoa, salt, and vinegar. Cook over moderate heat, stirring constantly, until the sugar dissolves and the mixture comes to a boil.

Stir in the evaporated milk and the butter. Continue cooking, stirring occasionally, until the mixture reaches the firm-ball stage (248°F on a candy thermometer). Pour the candy onto the prepared platter.

When the taffy is cool enough to handle, pull and fold it, with fingertips, until it is quite firm and light in color.

Pull the taffy into a long rope about $\frac{1}{2}$ inch in diameter. Using buttered kitchen scissors, cut the rope into 2-inch pieces. Wrap each piece in plastic wrap or waxed paper.

Christmas Confections

Popcorn balls and almond clusters, candied kumquats and walnut treats, fruit chews and butter mints—most of the confections in this section are easy to prepare, and, packaged with imagination, they all make very special, edible gifts.

Popcorn Balls

Popcorn balls are fun to make, especially if there are kids around to help. Make tiny balls and heap them in a bowl. Make medium-size or large balls, wrap each one in cellophane gathered at the top with a red or green ribbon, and hang them on the Christmas tree. About $\frac{1}{2}$ cup of unpopped corn should make the 6 cups of popped corn called for in this recipe.

  6 *cups popped corn*
  2 *cups shelled peanuts*
  $1\frac{1}{2}$ *tablespoons unsalted butter*
  $1\frac{1}{2}$ *cups firmly packed dark brown sugar*
  6 *tablespoons water*

Put the popped corn into a large bowl or pot. Add the peanuts. Mix well and set aside.

In a heavy saucepan, melt the butter over low heat. Add the sugar and water and continue cooking over low heat, stirring constantly, until the sugar is dissolved.

Increase the heat to moderate and boil the syrup, without stirring, until it reaches the soft-ball stage (238°F on a candy thermometer).

Slowly pour the hot syrup over the popped corn and peanuts, turning and mixing with a long-handled wooden spoon to coat all the kernels and nuts.

As soon as the mixture is cool enough to handle, shape it lightly into balls with buttered hands.

Let the popcorn balls dry thoroughly on waxed paper or a cookie sheet before wrapping them.

Almond Pecan Popcorn

This nutty popcorn has a light caramel glaze. It makes a wonderful gift, since it keeps well in airtight containers. A scant $\frac{3}{4}$ cup of unpopped corn should make the 8 cups of popped corn called for in this recipe.

> 2 cups pecan halves
> 2 cups blanched, whole almonds
> 8 cups popped corn
> 2 cups granulated sugar
> 1 cup light corn syrup
> $\frac{2}{3}$ cup water
> 2 cups unsalted butter, at room temperature

Preheat the oven to 350°F. Lightly oil a large bowl or pot. Lightly grease two cookie sheets with butter.

Spread the pecans and almonds on an ungreased cookie sheet in one layer. Toast them in the oven for about 10 minutes, or until they are lightly browned.

Combine the toasted nuts and the popped corn in the bowl or pot. Mix well.

In a large, heavy saucepan, combine the sugar, corn syrup, and water. Cook over high heat, stirring constantly, until the sugar is dissolved. Reduce the heat to moderate and cook, stirring frequently, until the mixture comes to a boil. Cut the butter into pieces, then add it and continue cooking, stirring constantly, until the mixture reaches the hard-crack stage (300°F on a candy thermometer).

Slowly pour the hot syrup over the nuts and popcorn, mixing and tossing with a long-handled wooden spoon to coat the nuts and popcorn with the caramel. Spread half the popcorn mixture in a thin layer on each cookie sheet.

When the mixture is completely cool, break it into small pieces.

Almond Clusters

These caramelized almonds look nice and taste wonderful. Store them in an airtight container between layers of waxed paper.

1½ cups unblanched almonds
1 cup granulated sugar

Lightly oil a large cookie sheet. Fill a large saucepan or bowl with cold water. Set aside.

In a heavy saucepan, combine the sugar and nuts. Cook over moderate heat, stirring constantly, until the sugar melts and is a dark caramel color. Dip the bottom of the pan quickly into the saucepan or bowl of cold water and remove it immediately.

Drop clusters of 3 or 4 nuts onto the prepared cookie sheet.

When the nuts are completely cool, transfer them to an airtight container.

Sugar and Spice Nuts

These nuts are a wonderful munch—and a great gift. Store them in an airtight container. Walnuts may be substituted for the pecans, or use half walnuts, half pecans.

2 cups firmly packed dark brown sugar
1 cup water
4 cups pecan halves
1 teaspoon ground cinnamon
$\frac{1}{4}$ teaspoon ground ginger

Grease two cookie sheets with butter.

In a heavy saucepan, combine the sugar and water. Cook over moderate heat, stirring constantly, until the sugar dissolves. Continue cooking, without stirring, until the syrup reaches the firm-ball stage (244°F on a candy thermometer).

Remove the pan from the heat. Stir in the nuts, cinnamon, and ginger. Continue to stir until the coating on the nuts begins to sugar.

Spread half the nuts on each prepared cookie sheet. Be sure they are all separated. Set aside until completely cool.

Walnut Treats

These sugary walnuts are flavored with lemon and orange. They will keep well in an airtight container.

1 cup granulated sugar
2 tablespoons water
2 tablespoons orange juice
2 tablespoons grated orange peel
2 tablespoons grated lemon peel
2 cups walnut halves

Grease a cookie sheet with butter.

In a heavy saucepan, combine the sugar, water, and orange juice. Cook over moderate heat, stirring constantly, until the syrup reaches the firm-ball stage (244°F on a candy thermometer).

Remove the pan from the heat and stir in the orange peel, lemon peel, and walnuts. Continue to stir until the syrup is creamy and the walnuts are well coated.

Spread the nuts on the prepared cookie sheet. Be sure they are all separated. Set aside until completely cool.

Fruit Chews

These chewy fruit-nut balls require no cooking and are full of good healthy ingredients. Store them in a cool, dry place or in the refrigerator.

$1\frac{1}{2}$ cups raisins
1 cup dried apricots
1 cup pitted dates
1 cup flaked coconut
1 cup finely chopped walnuts

In a food processor or blender, grind the raisins, apricots, and dates.

In a large mixing bowl, combine the ground fruit with the coconut and $\frac{1}{2}$ cup of the walnuts. Mix well.

Shape the mixture into thirty 1-inch balls.

Spread the remaining $\frac{1}{2}$ cup of chopped nuts on a plate. Roll the balls in the nuts, pressing the nuts firmly into them.

Walnut Date Slices

This chewy confection is quite easy to make. Pecans may be substituted for the walnuts. The slices keep best well-covered in the refrigerator, but serve them at room temperature.

3 cups granulated sugar
1 cup evaporated milk
1 cup finely chopped pitted dates
1 cup finely chopped walnuts

In a heavy saucepan, combine the sugar and milk. Cook over high heat, stirring constantly, until the sugar dissolves. Reduce heat to moderate and continue cooking, and stirring, until the mixture reaches the soft-ball stage (238°F on a candy thermometer).

Remove the pan from the heat and stir in the dates and the walnuts.

When the mixture is cool enough to handle, shape it into a roll, about 2 inches in diameter, using buttered hands. Wrap the roll in plastic wrap. Chill in the refrigerator overnight. Then, using a sharp knife, cut the roll into slices $\frac{1}{4}$ inch thick.

Taffy Apples

Commercially made taffy apples don't compare to the ones you make yourself. Be sure to use well-flavored, unblemished apples.

8 small or 6 large apples
2 cups granulated sugar
$\frac{1}{2}$ cup water
$\frac{1}{8}$ teaspoon cream of tartar
$\frac{1}{2}$ cup unsalted butter, cut into small pieces
1 teaspoon white vinegar
$\frac{1}{2}$ cup heavy cream

Push a lollypop stick or a skewer into the stem end of each apple. Liberally grease a cookie sheet with butter.

In a large, heavy saucepan, combine the sugar and the water. Cook over low heat, stirring constantly, until the sugar is dissolved.

Stir in the cream of tartar, butter, vinegar, and cream. Cook, stirring constantly, until the mixture reaches the soft-crack stage (290°F on a candy thermometer). Remove the pan from the heat.

Dip each apple into the syrup, then carefully place it on the prepared cookie sheet.

When the taffy has cooled completely, wrap each apple in plastic wrap.

Candied Orange Peel

This recipe makes a sugary, moist confection that keeps for many weeks in an airtight container. If you prefer candied grapefruit peel to orange, simply substitute the peel of 4 large grapefruits. Do not mix the peels in one batch. It's better to candy them separately.

8 large unblemished oranges
3 cups granulated sugar
1 cup water

Score the peel of each orange into eighths, then, using a blunt knife, pry the peel off the fruit. Scrape as much of the white pith (which can make the candy bitter) as possible from the inside of the peel. Cut the peel into strips.

Put the peel into a saucepan and add cold water to cover. Cook over low heat until the water comes to a boil. Remove the pan from the heat and drain the peel well. Repeat this process four more times, draining the peel thoroughly each time.

In a heavy saucepan, combine 2 cups of the sugar and the water. Cook over high heat, stirring constantly, until the sugar dissolves. Bring the syrup to a boil, add the drained peel, and cook over moderate heat, stirring constantly, until all the syrup is absorbed by the peel.

Turn the peel out onto an ungreased cookie sheet. Separate the peel. Let it cool.

Spread the remaining 1 cup of sugar on a large plate. Put a large sheet of waxed paper on a work surface.

When the peel is cool, roll it in the sugar, then put the pieces on the waxed paper to dry for about 2 hours.

Candied Kumquats

This sweet-sour little fruit has a unique flavor and makes a delightful confection. Use only firm, brightly colored kumquats.

4 cups kumquats
5 cups water
$3\frac{1}{2}$ cups granulated sugar
$\frac{1}{8}$ teaspoon cream of tartar

Wash the kumquats and, using a skewer or a tapestry needle, prick a hole in the stem end of each one.

Put the kumquats into a saucepan and add 4 cups of water. Cook over moderate heat until the water begins to boil. Reduce the heat and simmer the kumquats for 10 minutes.

Drain the kumquats in a colander, then spread them on paper towels to dry.

In a heavy saucepan, combine the remaining cup of water with 2 cups of the sugar. Cook over low heat, stirring constantly, until the sugar is dissolved. Stir in the cream of tartar. Increase the heat to moderate and cook, stirring constantly, until the syrup reaches the soft-ball stage (238°F on a candy thermometer).

Reduce the heat to low, add the kumquats, and let them simmer gently, stirring frequently, for 10 minutes.

Using a perforated spoon, remove the kumquats from the syrup and put them on wire racks to drain and cool.

Spread the remaining $1\frac{1}{2}$ cups of sugar on a plate.

When the kumquats are cool enough to handle, roll each one in the sugar. Return the kumquats to the wire racks to cool completely.

Butter Mints

These uncooked candies are surprisingly easy to make. They are traditionally served at the end of a meal. Store in an airtight container with waxed paper between the layers.

$\frac{1}{4}$ cup unsalted butter, at room temperature
1 pound confectioners' sugar
3 tablespoons heavy cream
1 teaspoon peppermint extract
   Red or green food coloring
   Granulated sugar

In a large mixing bowl, cream the butter and half of the confectioners' sugar. Add the cream, peppermint, and a few drops of food coloring and beat until the mixture is smooth. Using a wooden spoon or hands, work in the remaining confectioners' sugar until the mixture is smooth.

Put the candy on a large plate and cover it with a damp dish towel. Working with only a small amount of the candy at a time, shape it into sixty $\frac{1}{2}$-inch balls. If the mixture does become dry, mix in a few drops of water.

Flatten the balls with a fork dipped in granulated sugar. Let the mints dry on wire racks for 1 hour.

Coconut-Peanut Butter Bonbons

These easy-to-make little treats are baked in paper baking cups that are removed after the candy cools.

1 cup creamy peanut butter
½ cup granulated sugar
1 large egg
½ cup sweetened condensed milk
2 cups flaked coconut

Preheat the oven to 325°F. Place fifty 1¼-inch paper baking cups on a cookie sheet.

In a medium-size mixing bowl, combine the peanut butter, sugar, and egg. Stir until well blended. Press 1½ teaspoons of the mixture into the bottom of each baking cup.

In a small bowl, combine the milk and the coconut. Mix well, then put 1 teaspoonful of the mixture into each cup on top of the peanut butter mixture. Bake for 20 minutes, or until the tops of the bonbons are lightly browned. Cool on wire racks.

When the bonbons are completely cool, remove the baking cups.